GW01091524

Vegan Cookbook for Mum

Easy to prepare at home recipes for a balanced and healthy diet

By John Rincolls

© Copyright 2021 - All rights reserved.

The content contained within this book may not be reproduced, duplicated or transmitted without direct written permission from the author or the publisher.

Under no circumstances will any blame or legal responsibility be held against the publisher, or author, for any damages, reparation, or monetary loss due to the information contained within this book. Either directly or indirectly.

Legal Notice:

This book is copyright protected. This book is only for personal use. You cannot amend, distribute, sell, use, quote or paraphrase any part, or the content within this book, without the consent of the author or publisher.

Disclaimer Notice:

Please note the information contained within this document is for educational and entertainment purposes only. All effort has been executed to present accurate, up to date, and reliable, complete information. No warranties of any kind are declared or implied. Readers acknowledge that the author is not engaging in the rendering of legal, financial, medical or professional advice. The content within this book has been derived from various sources. Please consult a licensed professional before attempting any techniques outlined in this book. By reading this document, the reader agrees that under no circumstances is the author responsible for any losses, direct or indirect, which are incurred as a result of the use of information contained within this document, including, but not limited to, — errors, omissions, or inaccuracies.

Sommario

Introduction

Vegetarianism refers to a lifestyle that excludes the consumption of all forms of meat, including pork, chicken, beef, lamb, venison, fish and shells.

Depending on one's beliefs and expectations, vegetarianism has personal peculiarities, in fact there are some vegetarians who love to consume at least animal by-products and others who, instead, taking their beliefs to the extreme, prefer to eliminate even those and are called vegans.

Being vegetarian as well as respecting animals also has other important benefits such as reducing the risk of chronic disease and diabetes.

At this point I invite you to go in search of your favorite dish in our fantastic book, enjoy.

Main Course

Spicy Brown Rice with Vegan Chorizo

Ingredients

1 red onion,

chopped 6 garlic

cloves, minced 1

celery stalk, chopped

2 bell peppers, chopped

1 15 oz can diced

tomatoes 4 cups

vegetable broth

1 can water (I use the can of diced tomatoes to grab all the

leftoverflavor)

1/2 cup vegan Chorizo (Soyrizo),

crumbled 1 15 oz can Black Beans

2 tablespoons annatto

seeds 2 teaspoons cumin

1 tsp. cayenne pepper

1/2 cup uncooked brown

rice 1/4 teaspoon sea salt

Put all of the ingredients into slow cooker.

Cook on low for 8 hours or high for 4

hours.

Serve with toppings such as shredded vegan cheese, avocado, green onion and cilantro

Black Rice with Enoki Mushrooms

Ingredients

2 red onion,

chopped 7 garlic

cloves, minced

8 jalapeno peppers,
minced 1 tbsp. lemon
juice

4 cups vegetable broth

1 can water (I use the can of diced tomatoes to grab all the leftover flavor)

8 oz. dried mung beans

1 15 oz can enoki
mushrooms 2 tablespoons
garlic, minced 2 teaspoons
chili powder

1 tablespoon Thai chili garlic
paste 1/2 cup uncooked black
rice

1/4 teaspoon sea salt

Put all of the ingredients into slow cooker.
Cook on low for 8 hours or high for 4
hours.

Serve with toppings such as shredded vegan cheese, avocado, green onion and cilantro

Kidney Beans & Button Mushrooms with Pesto Sauce

Ingredien

ts 2 red
onions

7 garlic cloves

1 ancho chili,
minced 1 tbsp. lime
juice

4 cups vegetable broth

1 can water (I use the can of diced tomatoes to grab all the
leftover flavor)

8 oz. dried kidney beans

1 15 oz can button
mushrooms 3 tablespoons
pesto sauce

1 teaspoons dried basil, coarsely
chopped 1 tsp. dried Italian seasoning

1/2 cup uncooked
rice 1/4 teaspoon
sea salt

Put all of the ingredients into slow cooker.
Cook on low for 8 hours or high for 4
hours.

Serve with toppings such as shredded vegan cheese,
avocado, green onion and cilantro

Red Rice with Enoki Mushrooms and Tomatoes

Ingredients

1 red onion,

chopped 6 garlic

cloves, minced 1

celery stalk, chopped

2 bell peppers, chopped

1 15 oz can diced

tomatoes 4 cups

vegetable broth

1 can water (I use the can of diced tomatoes to grab all the leftover flavor)

8 oz. dried lentils

1 15 oz can enoki

mushrooms 2 tablespoons

garlic powder

2 teaspoons onion powder

1 tablespoon herbs de
Provence 1/2 cup uncooked
red rice

1/4 teaspoon sea salt

Put all of the ingredients into slow cooker.
Cook on low for 8 hours or high for 4
hours.

Serve with toppings such as shredded vegan cheese,
avocado, green onion and cilantro

Slow Cooked Quinoa and Tomatoes

Ingredients

1 red onion, chopped

1 white onion, chopped 8 garlic cloves, minced 1 tsp. shallot, minced

1 15 oz can diced tomatoes 4 cups vegetable broth

1 can water (I use the can of diced tomatoes to grab all the leftover flavor)

2 15 oz cans sliced porcini mushrooms 2 tablespoons chili powder

2 teaspoons cumin

1 tablespoon oregano
1/2 cup uncooked

quinoa 1/4 teaspoon

sea salt

Put all of the ingredients into slow cooker.

Cook on low for 8 hours or high for 4

hours.

Serve with toppings such as shredded vegan cheese,

avocado, green onion and cilantro

Brown Rice with Crimini Mushrooms and Jalapeno Pepper

Ingredients

2 red onion,
chopped 7 garlic
cloves, minced

8 jalapeno peppers,
minced 1 tbsp. lemon
juice

4 cups vegetable broth

1 can water (I use the can of diced tomatoes to grab all the
leftoverflavor)

1 15 oz can crimini
mushrooms 2 tablespoons
annatto seeds

2 teaspoons cumin

1 tsp. cayenne pepper

1/2 cup uncooked brown

rice 1/4 teaspoon sea salt

Put all of the ingredients into slow cooker.
Cook on low for 8 hours or high for 4
hours.

Serve with toppings such as shredded vegan cheese,
avocado, green onion and cilantro

Black Rice with Enoki Mushroom in Chimichurri

Ingredien

ts 2 red
onions

7 garlic cloves

1 ancho chili,
minced 1 tbsp. lime
juice

1 15 oz can diced
tomatoes 4 cups
vegetable broth

1 can water (I use the can of diced tomatoes to grab all the
leftover flavor)

1 8 oz can enoki
mushrooms 2 tablespoons
garlic, minced 2 teaspoons
chili powder

1 tablespoon chimichurri
1/2 cup uncooked black

rice 1/4 teaspoon sea salt

Put all of the ingredients into slow cooker.
Cook on low for 8 hours or high for 4
hours.

Serve with toppings such as shredded vegan cheese,
avocado, green onion and cilantro

Rice with Pesto Sauce and Button Mushrooms

Ingredients

1 red onion,
chopped 6 garlic
cloves, minced 1
celery stalk, chopped

2 bell peppers, chopped

1 15 oz can diced
tomatoes 4 cups
vegetable broth

1 can water (I use the can of diced tomatoes to grab all the
leftoverflavor)

1 15 oz can button
mushrooms 3 tablespoons
pesto sauce

1 teaspoons dried basil, coarsely
chopped 1 tsp. dried Italian seasoning

1/2 cup uncooked

rice1/4 teaspoon

sea salt

Put all of the ingredients into slow cooker.

Cook on low for 8 hours or high for 4

hours.

Serve with toppings such as shredded vegan cheese,

avocado,green onion and cilantro

Quinoa and Enoki Mushrooms

Ingredients

2 red onion,

chopped 7 garlic

cloves, minced

8 jalapeno peppers,
minced 1 tbsp. lemon
juice

4 cups vegetable broth

1 can water (I use the can of diced tomatoes to grab all the
leftoverflavor)

1 15 oz can enoki mushrooms

1 15 oz can button
mushrooms 2 tablespoons
chili powder

2 teaspoons cumin

1 tablespoon oregano
1/2 cup uncooked
quinoa 1/4 teaspoon
sea salt

Put all of the ingredients into slow cooker.
Cook on low for 8 hours or high for 4

hours.

Serve with toppings such as shredded vegan cheese, avocado,green onion and cilantro

Red Rice with Crimini and Button Mushrooms

Ingredients

2 red onion,
chopped 7 garlic
cloves, minced

1 tsp. scallions,
minced 1 tbsp. lemon
juice

4 cups vegetable broth

1 can water (I use the can of diced tomatoes to grab all the leftover flavor)

1 cup crimini
mushrooms 1 cup
button mushrooms

2 tablespoons garlic
powder 2 teaspoons onion
powder

1 tablespoon herbs de

Provence 1/2 cup uncooked
red rice

1/4 teaspoon sea salt

Put all of the ingredients into slow cooker.
Cook on low for 8 hours or high for 4
hours.

Serve with toppings such as shredded vegan cheese,
avocado, green onion and cilantro

Brown Rice with Vegan Chorizo and Ancho Chili

Ingredien
ts 2 red
onions

7 garlic cloves

1 ancho chili,
minced 1 tbsp. lime
juice

4 cups vegetable broth

1 can water (I use the can of diced tomatoes to grab all the
leftoverflavor)

1 cup crimini mushrooms

1/2 cup vegan Chorizo (Soyrizo),
crumbled 2 tablespoons annatto seeds

2 teaspoons cumin

1 tsp. cayenne pepper

1/2 cup uncooked brown

rice 1/4 teaspoon sea salt

Put all of the ingredients into slow cooker.
Cook on low for 8 hours or high for 4
hours.

Serve with toppings such as shredded vegan cheese,
avocado, green onion and cilantro

Veggie Pie

Ingredients

7 cups vegetables chopped into bite sized pieces as needed I used: brussel sprouts, frozen corn kernels, frozen peas, diced potatoes, baby carrots, and pre-sliced mushrooms

1/2 cup diced red onion4 cloves minced garlic

5-6 sprigs fresh thyme leaves removed1/4 cup flour

2 cups chicken stock1/4 cup cornstarch 1/4 cup heavy cream

salt and pepper to taste

1 frozen puff pastry sheet thawed2 tablespoons olive oil

Put the 7 cups of vegetables as needed to your slow cooker togetherwith the onion and garlic

Combine with the flour to coat well

Add the broth until well combined with the flour

Cover and cook on high heat for 3 and a half hours or low heat for 6and a half hours.

Combine cornstarch with 1/4 cup water until smooth and add this tothe slow cooker.

Add the coconut cream, cover, and return slow cooker.Cook on high for 15 minutes or until mixture thickens

Transfer to a baking dish and top with the thawed puff pastry sheet.Brush the olive oil over the top of pastry

Bake at 400 degrees F for about 10 minutes or until pastry turnsgolden brown.

Split Pea Celery and Leek Soup

Ingredients

1 16- oz package 1 lb dried green split peas, rinsed

1 large leek light green and white portion only, chopped andthoroughly cleaned

3 celery ribs diced

2 large carrots
diced 4 garlic clove
minced

1/4 cup chopped fresh
parsley6 cups vegetable
broth

1/2 t ground black
pepper1 tsp sea salt or
to taste 1 bay leaf

Pour all of the ingredients in a slow cooker and combine

thoroughly. Cover a cook on low heat for 7 and a half hours or high 3 and a halfhours.

Take out the bay leaf.

Soy Bean and Bell Pepper Soup

Ingredients

1 pound dry soy
beans4 cups
vegetable stock

1 yellow onion, finely chopped

1 green bell pepper, finely chopped

2 jalapeños, seeds removed and finely
chopped1 cup salsa or diced tomatoes

4 teaspoons minced garlic, about 4
cloves1 heaping tablespoon chili
powder

2 teaspoons ground
cumin2 teaspoons sea
salt

1 teaspoon ground pepper

1/2 teaspoon ground cayenne pepper (decrease or omit for a

mildersoup)

1/2 teaspoon smoked paprika

Avocado and cilantro for topping, if desired

Completely submerge the beans in water overnight and make surethere's an inch of water over the beans.

Drain the beans and rinse.

Put the beans, broth, onion, pepper, jalapeños, salsa, garlic, chili powder, cumin, salt, pepper, cayenne, and paprika in a slow cooker.Stir and combine thoroughly.

Cook on high heat for 6 hours, until beans are tender.

Blend half of the soup until smooth and bring it back to the pot.Top with avocado and cilantro.

Masala Brown ,Green and Pardina Lentils

Ingredients

1 red onion,
chopped 5 cloves
garlic, minced

1 tablespoon minced fresh ginger, or 1 teaspoon ground
gingerpowder

2¼ cups brown, green or pardina
lentils4 cups vegetable broth

1 15-ounce can diced San Marzano tomatoes, with their juices

¼ cup tomato paste

2 teaspoons tamarind paste (optional, adds a hint of
tartness)1 teaspoon honey

¾ teaspoon sea salt

1½ teaspoon garam
masalaA few shakes black
pepper 1 cup light

coconut milk

Side dish: Rice, quinoa, or another whole grain and fresh herbs

Put everything except for the coconut milk and side dish ingredientsin the slow cooker.

Combine thoroughly and cook on high for 3 and a half hours or onlow for 6 hours.

In the last hour, check if more liquid needs to be added.. When the lentils become more tender, add the coconut milk.Add this to the rice, quinoa and fresh herbs.

Slow Cooked Chick Peas and Vegetarian Sausage

Ingredients

2 teaspoons extra virgin olive oil

1 medium red onion, diced (about 2 cups)

4 medium cloves garlic, minced (about 2
teaspoons)2 teaspoons ground coriander

2 teaspoons ground
cumin 1/2 teaspoon
garam masala1/2
teaspoon ground ginger
1/4 teaspoon turmeric

1/4 teaspoon crushed red pepper
flakes1 teaspoon sea salt

1 (15-ounce) can diced
tomatoes2 tablespoons tomato
paste

1 cup vegetable stock

2 (15-ounce) cans chickpeas, drained and
rinsed 1/2 cup vegetarian grain meat
sausages, crumbled1 pound red potatoes, cut
into 1/2-inch dice

1 lime

Small bunch fresh
cilantroEquipment:

3-quart or larger slow cooker

Heat the olive oil in a large pan over medium heat.

Sauté the onion until softened and translucent. This takes about 5minutes.

Add in the garlic, coriander, cumin, garam masala, ground ginger,turmeric, red pepper flakes, and sea salt.

Cook and stir for 1 minute.

Add in the diced tomatoes, tomato paste, and vegetable broth.Combine and pour into the slow cooker.

Add the chickpeas and potatoes.

Cook on high heat for 4 1/2 hours or low for 9 hours, or until thepotatoes become fork-tender.

Serve in bowls and garnished with fresh cilantro and lime wedges.

Swiss Chard and White Bean Stew

Ingredients

2 pounds white beans (sorted and rinsed)2 large carrots, peeled and diced

3 large celery stalks, diced1 red onion, diced

6 cloves garlic, minced or chopped1 bay leaf

1 tsp. each: dried rosemary, thyme, oregano11 cups water

2 Tbsp. salt

Ground black pepper, to taste

1 large can (28 ounces) diced tomatoes5-6 cups chopped Swiss chard & kale Rice, polenta, or bread for serving

Combine beans, carrots, celery, onions, garlic, bay leaf and dried herbs.

Add the water.

Cook on high heat for 3 ½ hours, or low heat for 9 hours. Remove lid from slow cooker and season with salt and pepperAdd diced tomatoes.

Cook for another 1 hour and 15 min. or until beans get very soft. (Garnish with the chopped greens.

Serve with cooked rice, polenta, or with bread.

Red Potato and Baby Spinach Soup

Ingredients

5 cups low sodium vegetable stock

3 large red potatoes peeled and
chopped1 cup onion chopped

2   stalks   celery
chopped   4   cloves
garlic crushed 1 cup
heavy cream

1 tsp. dried
tarragon2 cups
baby spinach

6-8 Tbsp. sliced almonds

sea salt and ground black pepper to taste

Combine stock, sweet potatoes, onion, celery, and garlic to a 4-quartslow cooker.

Cook on low heat for 8 hours or until potatoes become soft. Add almond milk, tarragon, salt and pepper.

Blend this mixture for 1-2 minutes with an immersion blender untilsoup is smooth.

Add baby spinach & cover.

Let it rest for 20 minutes or until spinach becomes soft. Garnish with almonds and season with sea salt and pepper.

Faro and Kidney Bean Chili

Ingredients:

1 cup uncooked faro

1 medium red or yellow onion, peeled and diced8 cloves of garlic, minced

1 chipotle chili in adobo sauce, chopped

2 (15 ounce) cans dark red kidney beans, rinsed and drained (**seebelow for substitution ideas)

2 (15 ounce) cans tomato sauce

2 (14 ounce) cans diced tomatoes

1 (15 ounce) can light red kidney beans, rinsed and drained1 (4 ounce) can chopped red chilies

4 cups vegetable broth

1 cup beer (or you can just add extra vegetable broth)2 Tablespoons chili powder

1 Tablespoon ground

cumin1 teaspoon sea salt

1 teaspoon honey

1/2 teaspoon black pepper

Combine all of the ingredients in a slow cooker and stir thoroughly. Cook on high for 3 ½ hours or on low heat for 7 hours until the beans are soft.

Taste, and add more salt and pepper if necessary. Garnish with toppings.

Refrigerate for 3 days or freeze for 3 months.

Grilled Zucchinis and Crimini Mushrooms

Ingredients

2 zucchinis, cut into 1/2-inch slices 2 red bell peppers, cut into chunks 1/2 pound fresh crimini mushrooms

1/2 pound cherry tomatoes1 red onion, cut into 1/2-inch-thick slices1/2 cup olive oil

sea salt to taste

freshly ground black pepper to taste

Preheat your grill for medium-high heatOil the grate.

Mix the zucchinis, green bell peppers, mushrooms, tomatoes, andonion in a bowl.

Drizzle some olive oil over vegetables and toss them to coat.Season with sea salt and pepper.

Grill the vegetables for 4 minutes per side.

Grilled Zucchini and Cremini Mushrooms with Balsamic Glaze

Ingredients

3 yellow bell peppers, seeded and halved

3 summer squash (about 1 pound total), sliced lengthwise into 1/2-inch-thick rectangles

3 zucchini (about 12 ounces total), sliced lengthwise into 1/2-inch-thick rectangles

3 eggplant (12 ounces total), sliced lengthwise into 1/2-inch-thickrectangles

12 cremini mushrooms

1 bunch (1-pound) asparagus, trimmed12 green onions, roots cut off

6 tablespoons olive oil

Salt and freshly ground black pepper3 tablespoons balsamic

vinegar

4 garlic cloves, minced

1 teaspoon chopped fresh parsley
leaves1 teaspoon chopped fresh basil
leaves

1/2 teaspoon finely chopped fresh rosemary leaves

Preheat your grill for medium-high heat

Lightly brush the vegetables with 1/4 cup of
the oilSeason the vegetables with salt and
pepper.

Working in batches, grill them until tender.

Combine the 2 tablespoons of oil, balsamic vinegar, garlic,
parsley,basil, and rosemary in a bowl.

Season with salt and pepper.

Drizzle the vinaigrette over the vegetables.

Grilled Asparagus Carrots and Squash

Ingredients

Marinade Ingredients

1/4 cup extra virgin olive oil2 tablespoons honey

4 teaspoons balsamic vinegar1 teaspoon dried oregano

1 teaspoon garlic powder

1/8 teaspoon rainbow peppercornsSea salt

Vegetable Ingredients

1 pound fresh asparagus, trimmed

3 small carrots, cut in half lengthwise

1 large sweet green pepper, cut into 1-inch strips

1 medium yellow summer squash, cut into 1/2-inch

slices 1 medium yellow onion, cut into wedges

Combine the marinade ingredients.

Combine the 3 tablespoons marinade and vegetables in a bag. Marinate 1 1/2 hours at room temperature or overnight in the refrigerator.

Grill the vegetables over medium heat for 8-12 minutes or until tender.

Sprinkle the remaining marinade.

Grilled Zucchini and Red Onions in Ranch Dressing

Ingredients

2 large zucchini , cut lengthwise into ½ inch slabs

2 large red onions, cut into ½ inch rings but don't separate intoindividual rings

2 tbsp. extra virgin olive

oil2 tbsp. ranch dressing
mix

Lightly brush each side of the vegetables with olive
oil.Season with the ranch dressing mix

Grill over 4 minutes over medium heat or until tender.

Grilled Sweet Corns and Portobello

Ingredients

2 large Sweet Corns, cut
lengthwise 5 pcs. Portobello,
rinsed and drained

Marinade Ingredients:

6 tbsp. extra virgin olive
oilSea salt, to taste

3 tbsp. distilled white
vinegar1 tsp. Dijon
mustard

Marinate the vegetable with the dressing or marinade
ingredients for15 to 30 min.

Grill for 4 minutes over medium heat or until the vegetable
becomestender.

Grilled Marinated Eggplant and Zucchini

Ingredients

2 large Eggplants, cut lengthwise and cut in half2 large Zucchinis, cut lengthwise and cut in half

Marinade Ingredients:

6 tbsp. extra virgin olive oilSea salt, to taste

3 tbsp. distilled white vinegar1 tsp. pesto sauce

Marinate the vegetable with the dressing or marinade ingredients for15 to 30 min.

Grill for 4 minutes over medium heat or until the vegetable becomestender.

Grilled Bell Pepper and Broccolini

Ingredients

2 Green Bell Peppers, cut in
half10 Broccolini Florets

Marinade Ingredients:

6 tbsp. extra virgin olive
oilSea salt, to taste

3 tbsp. distilled white vinegar

1 tsp. sun-dried tomato pesto sauce

Marinate the vegetable with the dressing or marinade
ingredients for15 to 30 min.

Grill for 4 minutes over medium heat or until the vegetable
becomestender.

Grilled Cauliflower and Brussel Sprouts

Ingredients

10 Cauliflower florets

10 pcs. Brussel
Sprouts

Marinade Ingredients:

6 tbsp. extra virgin olive
oilSea salt, to taste

3 tbsp. distilled white
vinegar1 tsp. mayonnaise

Marinate the vegetable with the dressing or marinade ingredients for15 to 30 min.

Grill for 4 minutes over medium heat or until the vegetable becomestender.

Grilled Corn and Crimini Mushrooms

Ingredients

2 Corns, cut lengthwise

10 Crimini Mushrooms, rinsed and drained

Marinade Ingredients:

6 tbsp. extra virgin olive
oilSea salt, to taste

3 tbsp. distilled white
vinegar1 tsp. Dijon
mustard

Marinate the vegetable with the dressing or marinade
ingredients for15 to 30 min.

Grill for 4 minutes over medium heat or until the vegetable
becomestender.

Grilled Eggplant, Zucchini and Corn

Ingredients

2 large Eggplants, cut lengthwise and cut in half2 large Zucchinis, cut lengthwise and cut in half2 Corns, cut lengthwise

Marinade Ingredients:

6 tbsp. extra virgin olive oilSea salt, to taste

3 tbsp. distilled white vinegar1 tsp. mayonnaise

Marinate the vegetable with the dressing or marinade ingredients for15 to 30 min.

Grill for 4 minutes over medium heat or until the vegetable becomestender.

Grilled Zucchini and Pineapple

Ingredients

2 large zucchini , cut lengthwise into ½ inch slabs

2 large red onions, cut into ½ inch rings but don't separate into individual rings

1 medium Pineapple, cut into 1/2 inch slices10 Green Beans

Marinade Ingredients:

6 tbsp. extra virgin olive oilSea salt, to taste

3 tbsp. distilled white vinegar1 tsp. honey

Marinate the vegetable with the dressing or marinade ingredients for15 to 30 min.

Grill for 4 minutes over medium heat or until the vegetable becomestender.

Grilled Portobello and Eggplant

Ingredients

3 pcs. Portobello, rinsed and drained

2 pcs. Eggplant, cut lengthwise and cut in
half2 pcs. Zucchini, cut lengthwise and cut
in half6 pcs. Asparagus

Marinade Ingredients:

6 tbsp. extra virgin olive
oilSea salt, to taste

3 tbsp. distilled white
vinegar1 tsp. English
mustard

Marinate the vegetable with the dressing or marinade
ingredients for15 to 30 min.

Grill for 4 minutes over medium heat or until the vegetable
becomestender.

Grilled Asparagus and Mushrooms

Ingredients

6 pcs. Crimini mushrooms, rinsed and drained2 pcs. Eggplant, cut lengthwise and cut in half2 pcs. Zucchini, cut lengthwise and cut in half 6 pcs. Asparagus

Dressing Ingredients

6 tbsp. extra virgin olive oilSea salt, to taste

3 tbsp. apple cider vinegar1 tbsp. honey

1 tsp. Egg-free mayonnaise

Marinate the vegetable with the dressing or marinade ingredients for15 to 30 min.

Grill for 4 minutes over medium heat or until the vegetable becomestender.

Grilled Japanese Eggplant and Shitake Mushroom

Ingredients

Corns, cut lengthwise

2 pcs. Japanese Eggplant, cut lengthwise and cut in
half3 Shitake Mushrooms, rinsed and drained

Dressing
Ingredients6 tbsp.
olive oil

Sea salt, to taste

3 tbsp. white wine
vinegar 1 tsp. Egg-free
mayonnaise

Marinate the vegetable with the dressing or marinade
ingredients for15 to 30 min.

Grill for 4 minutes over medium heat or until the vegetable

becomestender.

Grilled Japanese Eggplant Bell Peppers and Broccolini

Ingredients

2 Green Bell Peppers, cut in
half10 Broccolini Florets

2 pcs. Japanese Eggplant, cut lengthwise and cut in half

Dressing
Ingredients6 tbsp.
sesame oil Sea
salt, to taste

3 tbsp. distilled white
vinegar1 tsp. mayonnaise

Marinate the vegetable with the dressing or marinade
ingredients for15 to 30 min.

Grill for 4 minutes over medium heat or until the vegetable
becomestender.

Grilled Cauliflower and Brussel Sprouts

Ingredients

10 Cauliflower florets

10 pcs. Brussel Sprouts

Dressing
Ingredients6 tbsp.
sesame oil

3 tbsp. distilled white
vinegar1 tsp. soy sauce

1 tsp. Hoi Sin Sauce

Marinate the vegetable with the dressing or marinade
ingredients for15 to 30 min.

Grill for 4 minutes over medium heat or until the vegetable
becomestender.

Grilled Japanese Bell Pepper and Cauliflower Recipe with Balsamic Glaze

Ingredients

2 Yellow Bell Peppers, cut in half lengthwise10 Cauliflower Florets

2 pcs. Japanese Eggplant, cut lengthwise and cut in half

Dressing Ingredients

6 tbsp. extra virgin olive oilSea salt, to taste

3 tbsp. Balsamic vinegar1 tsp. Dijon mustard

Marinate the vegetable with the dressing or marinade ingredients for15 to 30 min.

Grill for 4 minutes over medium heat or until the vegetable

becomestender.

Grilled Broccoli and Zucchini Recipe

Ingredients

2 large Eggplants, cut lengthwise and cut in half1 large Zucchini, cut lengthwise and cut in half 5 Broccoli Florets

Marinade Ingredients:

6 tbsp. extra virgin olive oilSea salt, to taste

3 tbsp. distilled white vinegar1 tsp. mayonnaise

Marinate the vegetable with the dressing or marinade ingredients for15 to 30 min.

Grill for 4 minutes over medium heat or until the vegetable becomestender.

Grilled Eggplant and Yellow Bell Peppers

Ingredients

2 Yellow Bell Peppers, cut in

half10 Broccolini Florets

2 pcs. Eggplant, cut lengthwise and cut in half

Dressing

Ingredients6 tbsp.

olive oil

Sea salt, to taste

3 tbsp. white wine

vinegar1 tsp. mustard

Marinate the vegetable with the dressing or marinade

ingredients for15 to 30 min.

Grill for 4 minutes over medium heat or until the vegetable

becomestender.

Grilled Portobello Asparagus and Pineapple

Ingredients

3 pcs. Portobello, rinsed and drained

2 pcs. Eggplant, cut lengthwise and cut in half2 pcs. Zucchini, cut lengthwise and cut in half6 pcs. Asparagus

1 medium Pineapple, cut into 1/2 inch slices10 Green Beans

Dressing Ingredients

6 tbsp. extra virgin olive oilSea salt, to taste

3 tbsp. apple cider vinegar1 tbsp. honey

1 tsp. mayonnaise

Marinate the vegetable with the dressing or marinade ingredients for15 to 30 min.

Grill for 4 minutes over medium heat or until the vegetable becomestender.

Grilled Collard Greens and Portobello Mushrooms

Ingredients

1 bunch of collard greens

5 pcs. Portobello mushrooms, rinsed and drained10 Asparagus spears

Dressing
Ingredients6 tbsp.
olive oil

Sea salt, to taste

3 tbsp. white wine
vinegar 1 tsp. Egg-free
mayonnaise

Marinate the vegetable with the dressing or marinade ingredients for15 to 30 min.

Grill for 4 minutes over medium heat or until the vegetable becomestender.

Brussel Sprouts and Endives

Ingredients

10 Cauliflower florets

10 pcs. Brussel

Sprouts1 bunch of

endives

Dressing

Ingredients6 tbsp.

olive oil

Sea salt, to taste

3 tbsp. white wine

vinegar 1 tsp. Egg-free

mayonnaise

Marinate the vegetable with the dressing or marinade

ingredients for15 to 30 min.

Grill for 4 minutes over medium heat or until the vegetable

becomestender.

Red Cabbage and Onion in Ranch Dressing

Ingredients

1 Red cabbage

2 large red onions, cut into ½ inch rings but don't separate intoindividual rings

2 tbsp. extra virgin olive
oil2 tbsp. ranch dressing
mix

Marinate the vegetable with the dressing or marinade ingredients for15 to 30 min.

Grill for 4 minutes over medium heat or until the vegetable becomestender.

Grilled Green Bean and Microgreens in Balsamic Vinaigrette

Ingredients

1 bunch of
microgreens10 Green
Beans Dressing
Ingredients

6 tbsp. extra virgin olive
oilSea salt, to taste

3 tbsp. Balsamic
vinegar1 tsp. mustard

Marinate the vegetable with the dressing or marinade ingredients for15 to 30 min.

Grill for 4 minutes over medium heat or until the vegetable becomestender.

Grilled Broccolini Asparagus and Eggplants

Ingredients

1 large Eggplants, cut lengthwise and cut in half1 bunch of turnip greens

10 Asparagus spears

10 Broccolini Florets

Marinade Ingredients:

6 tbsp. extra virgin olive oilSea salt, to taste

3 tbsp. distilled white vinegar1 tsp. Dijon mustard

Marinate the vegetable with the dressing or marinade ingredients for15 to 30 min.

Grill for 4 minutes over medium heat or until the vegetable becomestender.

Grilled Broccolini and Turnip Greens

Ingredients

1 bunch of turnip

greens8 Broccolini

Florets

Dressing Ingredients6

tbsp. sesame oil Sea

salt, to taste

3 tbsp. distilled white

vinegar1 tsp. Egg-free

mayonnaise

Marinate the vegetable with the dressing or marinade

ingredients for15 to 30 min.

Grill for 4 minutes over medium heat or until the vegetable

becomestender.

Grilled Rutabaga and Mustard Greens

Ingredients

1 medium Rutabaga, peeled and cut in half lengthwise

1 large red onion, cut into ½ inch rings but don't separate into individual rings

1 bunch of mustard greens

Dressing
Ingredients 6 tbsp.
olive oil

Sea salt, to taste

3 tbsp. white wine
vinegar 1 tsp. English
mustard

Marinate the vegetable with the dressing or marinade ingredients for 15 to 30 min.

Grill for 4 minutes over medium heat or until the vegetable

becomestender.

Grilled Green Cabbage in Apple Cider Vinaigrette

Ingredients

1 large parsnip, peeled and cut lengthwise

5 pcs. Portobello mushrooms, rinsed and drained1 Green cabbage, cut in half

Dressing Ingredients

6 tbsp. extra virgin olive oilSea salt, to taste

3 tbsp. apple cider vinegar1 tbsp. honey

1 tsp. Egg-free mayonnaise

Marinate the vegetable with the dressing or marinade ingredients for15 to 30 min.

Grill for 4 minutes over medium heat or until the vegetable becomestender.

Grilled Turnips with Broccoli

Ingredients

10 Broccoli florets

1 large turnips, peeled and cut
lengthwise1 Red cabbage, cut in half

Dressing
Ingredients6 tbsp.
olive oil

Sea salt, to taste

3 tbsp. white wine
vinegar 1 tsp. Egg-free
mayonnaise

Marinate the vegetable with the dressing or marinade
ingredients for15 to 30 min.

Grill for 4 minutes over medium heat or until the vegetable

becomestender.

Grilled Parsnip and Rutabaga

Ingredients

1 large parsnip, peeled and cut lengthwise

1 medium Rutabaga, peeled and cut in half lengthwise

2 large red onions, cut into ½ inch rings but don't separate intoindividual rings

Marinade Ingredients:

6 tbsp. extra virgin olive oilSea salt, to taste

3 tbsp. distilled white vinegar1 tsp. Dijon mustard

Marinate the vegetable with the dressing or marinade ingredients for15 to 30 min.

Grill for 4 minutes over medium heat or until the vegetable becomestender.

Grilled Turnip and Beetroots

Ingredients

1 large turnip, peeled and cut
lengthwise1 large carrot, peeled and
cut lengthwise

1 medium Beetroot , peeled and cut in half lengthwise

Dressing
Ingredients6 tbsp.
sesame oil Sea
salt, to taste

3 tbsp. distilled white
vinegar1 tsp. Egg-free
mayonnaise

Marinate the vegetable with the dressing or marinade
ingredients for15 to 30 min.

Grill for 4 minutes over medium heat or until the vegetable becomestender.

Conclusion

We have come to the end of this cookbook, but I will be writing more soon.

Did you enjoy trying these new and delicious vegetarian recipes?

I sure hope so.

One piece of advice I would like to give you is that in addition to trying these fantastic vegetarian recipes and reaping the benefits is to always do some physical activity to accentuate the benefits.

A perfect combination to maintain physical and emotional well-being.

I send you a big hug and hope to continue to keep you company with our vegetarian recipes.

See you soon.

CPSIA information can be obtained
at www.ICGtesting.com
Printed in the USA
BVHW090214210421
605389BV00007B/1895